IDEAS

A SIMPLE GUIDE FOR KIDS

TO LEARN ABOUT ANYTHING

CHERYL PETERSON, PH.D.

Dedicated to the many students
who have inspired me with their IDEAS
and to one of the best group of students
I've ever had the pleasure to teach:
Brooks, Leo, Emily, Lily and Drew,
& my awesome teaching assistant, Laura.

IMAGINE POSSIBILITIES & IDENTIFY A TOPIC

DEVELOP A LEARNING PLAN & QUESTIONS

EXPLORE ANSWERS & CONNECTIONS

ANNOUNCE TO AN AUDIENCE

SELF-REFLECT & EVALUATE

This is my idea, I thought.
No one knows it like I do.
And it's ok if it's different, and weird, and maybe a little crazy.
I decided to protect it, to care for it.
I fed it good food. I worked with it, I played with it.
But most of all I gave it my attention.
My idea grew and grew. And so did my love for it.
From: What do you do with an idea?
By Kobi Yamaha, 2013

TABLE OF CONTENTS

What is an IDEAS project?..1
Project Guide..2
Imagine Possibilities and Identify a Topic
    Getting Started...3
    Set Purpose with Stories...4
    Topic Brainstorm..5
    100 Club Card...6
    Criteria Matrix...7
    Criteria Matrix Sample..8
Develop a Learning Plan & Questions
    Getting Started...9
    Learning Plan Map..10
    Develop Questions...11
    Question Brainstorm...12
    Types of Questions..13
    Question Focus..14
Explore Answers and Connections
    Getting Started...15
    Collect Resources...16
    Resource Guidelines...17
    Resources..18
    Note-taking...19
    Nutshelling Practice..20
    Collection Grid...21
    Notecards...22
    Make Connections...23
    Bubble Brainstorm 24

TABLE OF CONTENTS

Announce to an Audience
 Getting Started..25
 Audience Brainstorm...26
 Product Possibilities..27
 Sharing Plan...28
 Solicit Feedback...29
 Feedback Form...30
Self-Reflect and Evaluate
 Getting Started...31
 Evaluate Using Criteria...32
 Self-Reflect..33
 My Epic Fails..34
Scaffolds...35
 Change the Lightbulb...36
 Playlist..37
 Work Tracker..38
DASH
 Getting Started...39
 Develop a Plan...40
 Announce to an Audience...41
 Self-reflect...42
 Highlight...43

TABLE OF CONTENTS

Stick It Research

Getting Started...44

Hook Your Readers...45

Thesis Statement Rules...46

Clever Conclusions..47

Introduction Planning Page..48

Body Planning Page – 1..49

Body Planning Page – 2..50

Conclusion Planning Page...51

Transitions...52

Putting It All Together..53

About the Author...54

Resources..55

WHAT IS AN IDEAS PROJECT?

Learning is fun. This handbook will guide you through a simple process to help you learn about anything you want. There are five steps based on the acronym IDEAS. Using this process, you imagine possibilities & identify a topic, develop a learning plan & questions, explore answers & connections, announce to an audience, and self-reflect & evaluate.

I believe learning is based on three key components: play, practice and purpose. Keeping these in mind can enhance your learning process. Play initiates learning and provides energy. Play in this case is more spirit and energy than an activity. Approaching an IDEAS project with a spirit of playfulness helps you learn. As you work through the project, much of what you will be doing and learning will be new. By practicing new skills and ways of thinking you will become a better learner. It's helpful to remember failure and mistakes are part of practice. You can use the epic fail worksheet on page 34 to record and celebrate your mistakes. There aren't correct ways to learn. You need to create this practice using the steps provided and your own ideas and experience. This is where purpose is important. It's helpful to think about why you are doing an IDEAS project. Maybe you have an upcoming trip and want to learn about what to do or where to go. Perhaps you have a desire to grow your own food, but you don't know how. Or maybe you just want to have fun learning about something interesting to you. Whatever your reason for wanting to learn something, IDEAS can guide you through the process.

Use the project guide to keep track of what you are doing and learning. Work through each step of the IDEAS process using the provided guides and worksheets. The scaffold section at the end includes extra supports to help with different needs.

I hope you enjoy IDEAS! I would love to hear about your project. Share it with me at

drcherylpeterson.com

PROJECT GUIDE

TRACKING PROGRESS

STEP	TARGET	EVIDENCE	DATE
IMAGINE POSSIBILITIES AND IDENTIFY A TOPIC	I explore multiple topic ideas and select one based on criteria.		
DEVELOP A LEARNING PLAN AND QUESTIONS	I develop an inquiry based learning plan with questions which address the topic in deep and complex ways.		
EXPLORE ANSWERS AND CONNECTIONS	I explore answers using multiple resources and connect ideas in unique and meaningful ways.		
ANNOUNCE TO AN AUDIENCE	I identify an appropriate audience and share my learning in an engaging way with that audience.		
SELF-REFLECT & EVALUATE	I reflect on what I have learned about the process of learning and about my topic.		

IMAGINE POSSIBILITIES & IDENTIFY A TOPIC

GETTING STARTED

An IDEAS project starts with a thought, question or wondering. It is something you want to know more about. One of my favorite ways to start an IDEAS project is by reading the book, What Do You Do with an IDEA? by Kobi Yamada. It is a creative story about a child who learns to care for and appreciate an idea. This IDEAS process will help you care for your ideas and grow them into something you can share. Imagine possibilities and identify a topic has 3 parts: a warm-up, topic brainstorm, and select a topic.

WARM-UP: SET PURPOSE WITH STORIES

This is a great warm up activity to help you imagine possibilities and explore what you might choose for an IDEAS project. Use this page to capture stories and ideas about things you are interested in and might want to learn about. You can make it even more fun with pictures and colored markers or pencils.

TOPIC BRAINSTORM: 100 CHALLENGE

Once you have all of your ideas flowing, it's time for the Topic Brainstorm. Start by identifying a topic. Brainstorm things you are interested in learning about. Try to think of many, varied and unusual ideas. Write them down as fast as you can. Don't worry if it's a good idea or not, just go for LOTS of ideas. Ask other people for ideas. Write down some more. 100 might seem like a lot, but it gets you playing with IDEAS and helps you find something you are really excited to learn about.

SELECT A TOPIC: CRITERIA MATRIX

Now it's time to pick your IDEAS topic. One might stand out to you as something you want to learn about right now. If you are having trouble picking something, you can use a criteria matrix. Follow the directions on the page and use the sample to help you get started.

IMAGINE POSSIBILITIES & IDENTIFY A TOPIC

SET PURPOSE WITH STORIES

Share stories about what ideas and topics are important or interesting to you. Use pictures or words to capture your ideas.

IMAGINE POSSIBILITIES & IDENTIFY A TOPIC

TOPIC BRAINSTORM

Keeping your stories in mind, brainstorm topics to learn about. Capture them as quickly as you can without judging or editing. Play with it and have fun! Collect 100 to join the 100 club.

1.	26.	51.	76.
2.	27.	52.	77.
3.	28.	53.	78.
4.	29.	54.	79.
5.	30.	55.	80.
6.	31.	56.	81.
7.	32.	57.	82.
8.	33.	58.	83.
9.	34.	59.	84.
10.	35.	60.	85.
11.	36.	61.	86.
12.	37.	62.	87.
13.	38.	63.	88.
14.	39.	64.	89.
15.	40.	65.	90.
16.	41.	66.	91.
17.	42.	67.	92.
18.	43.	68.	93.
19.	44.	69.	94.
20.	45.	70.	95.
21.	46.	71.	96.
22.	47.	72.	97.
23.	48.	73.	98.
24.	49.	74.	99.
25.	50.	75.	100.

IMAGINE POSSIBILITIES & IDENTIFY A TOPIC

100 CLUB

You did it! You identified 100 things to learn about. Use the following worksheets to pick which topic you want to learn more about right now. You can come back to your list for more ideas later. Use this sheet to make your very own official 100 club membership card.

FRONT
Add your name and a photo

IDEAS 100 CLUB

_____

OFFICIAL MEMBER OF THE IDEAS 100 CLUB

BACK

IDEAS 100 CLUB

IMAGINE POSSIBILITIES AND IDENTIFY A TOPIC

DEVELOP A LEARNING PLAN AND QUESTIONS

EXPLORE ANSWERS AND CONNECTIONS

ANNOUNCE TO AN AUTHENTIC AUDIENCE

SELF-REFLECT AND EVALUATE

IMAGINE POSSIBILITIES & IDENTIFY A TOPIC

CRITERIA MATRIX

Identify criteria you can use to judge your ideas and list them in the top row. Select your top 5 topic ideas. List them in the first column. For each criteria rank the topics 1–5 with 5 being the best. Total your rows. Which topic scored the highest? This is your IDEAS project topic.

Criteria

Topics					Totals

My IDEAS project topic:

IMAGINE POSSIBILITIES & IDENTIFY A TOPIC

CRITERIA MATRIX SAMPLE

Here is a sample criteria matrix. I used the criteria interesting, hands-on, experts available and lots of information. I put these on the top of the chart. Then I picted my five best ideas and listed them on the side. I looked at my first criteria, interesting, and numbered each of my topics from 1-5 with 5 being the best. Horses were the most interesting to me. I did the same thing for each of the criteria and totaled up the rows. Gardening is the best topic based on my criteria. Horses were a pretty close second so that might be a good topic too. The criteria matrix is just a guide to help you pick a topic. If you really want to learn about something and it didn't score high, you can still pick it or do it next time.

Criteria

Topics	Interesting	Hands-on	Experts I can talk to	Lots of info	Totals
Gardening	4	5	4	5	18
Bee Keeping	2	4	1	1	8
Raising Chickens	3	3	3	2	11
Baseball	1	2	2	4	9
Horses	5	1	5	3	14

My IDEAS project topic: Gardening

 # DEVELOP A LEARNING PLAN

GETTING STARTED

How will you learn about your topic? Where will you find information? Who can you talk to that is an expert? What sort of experiments can you do? These types of questions are important in developing a learning plan. A learning plan is like a map. It can serve as a guide as you begin to learn about your topic. Use the guide on the following page to start building your learning map.

BOOKS are a great resource for your learning plan. Check out your local library and find out if there are any books on your topic. Talk to the librarian. Ask for help finding resources about your topic. Write the title of these books on your learning map.

PEOPLE can be another resource. Who can you talk to? Do you know any experts? Is there someone else who is interested in the topic that might want to talk about it with you? Add these people to you learning plan. Ask trusted adults if they know anyone you should talk to about your topic.

PLACES TO VISIT. Where can you go to learn more about your topic? Museums, nature centers, or zoos might be places you want to visit. Sometimes you can even take a virtual visit using the internet if where you want to go is too far or not possible. Add some places to visit to your learning plan.

EXPERIMENTS or investigations might be another way to learn about your topic. You can use this space to list any hands-on activity you might do to learn more about your topic.

After you have a learning plan, start exploring your topic. Keep track of the new things you learn and begin developing questions to further your research.

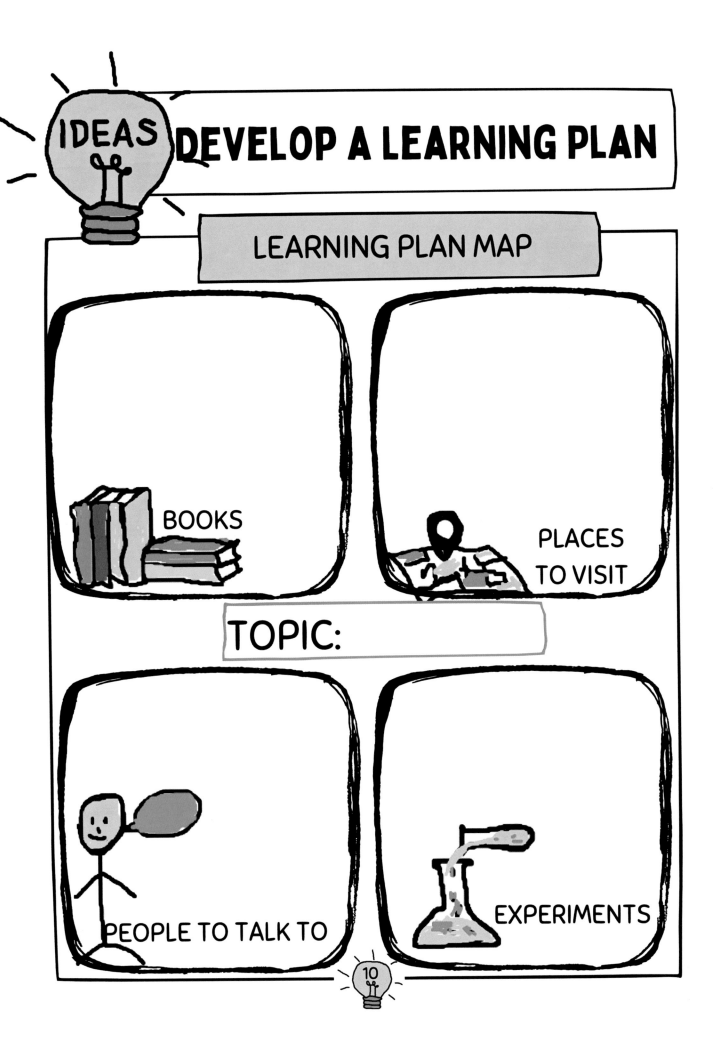

DEVELOP A LEARNING PLAN

DEVELOP QUESTIONS

Develop your topic by asking questions. Make a list of questions you are curious about. Let your ideas flow. Ask as many questions as you can about your topic. Look over your questions. What questions really make you think about the topic. What questions do you really want to know? Choose your top three questions to get started. Develop questions has 3 parts: question brainstorm, types of questions and question focus.

QUESTION BRAINSTORM
Just like in the topic brainstorm, you want to let your ideas flow. Sticky notes are a useful tool for this step. You can write one question on each sticky note and then move them around and see if any of your questions go together. They can help you organize your thoughts and really think about what you want to learn about.

TYPES OF QUESTIONS
This worksheet is useful if you are having trouble thinking of questions or if you just want to explore asking different types of questions. Use the sample questions as guides and try to come up with different types of questions about your topic.

QUESTION FOCUS
After spending some time thinking about questions, you should have some questions you want to focus on. This is a good time to reflect on your purpose. Why are these questions important to you? How will learning about this help you? Will you be able to use what you learned to make the world better? Use the questions focus worksheet to identify your top 3 questions and reflect on why they are important to you.

IDEAS DEVELOP A LEARNING PLAN

QUESTION BRAINSTORM

What do you wonder about your topic? What do you want to know or figure out? Use sticky notes to brainstorm as many questions as you can. Then see if any of your questions can be grouped together. Use this page to record your question brainstorm.

DEVELOP A LEARNING PLAN

TYPES OF QUESTIONS

Types of Questions	My Questions
What if....? Questions • What if cell phones had not been invented? • What if water didn't freeze?	
Quantity Questions • What are all the ways you an think of to play sports? • Can you list reasons why the invention of cars was a good idea?	
Compare/Contrast Questions • How are horses and zebras alike? • Can you contrast a toy car with an automobile?	
Point of View Questions • Would you rather win a million dollars or go to the moon? • Would you rather take the bus or carpool?	
How come....? Questions • How come the state of Hawaii has interstate highways? • How come we drive on parkways & park in driveways?	

13

Adapted from: Johnson, N. (1999). The Quick Question Workbook. Pieces of Learning. Marian, IL.

DEVELOP A LEARNING PLAN

What are the top 3 inquiry questions you have about your topic?

1 _____
_____

2 _____
_____

3 _____
_____

Why are these questions important to you?

What do you hope to learn?

What materials or resources will you need?

How can others support your project?

EXPLORE ANSWERS & CONNECTIONS

GETTING STARTED

Exploring answers and connections is a bit messy. It's more than just finding answers to your questions. It's collecting and organizing information so it makes sense to you and the audience with whom you share it. It's helpful to think of it as curating information, much like a museum curator collects artifacts and creates exhibits. You might start by looking for answers to your questions or by reading and learning about your topic from a variety of resources. Exploring answers and connections has 3 parts: collecting resources, note taking and connection making.

COLLECTING RESOURCES
One of the first steps to exploring answers and connections is to locate sources of information. You might begin by finding books or internet resources about your topic. Libraries and assistance from a librarians are often good starting points. You might also look for experts to interview and other sources of print material including encyclopedias, magazines, textbooks and informational articles. You might also find digital material using the internet. Make sure you use trusted sources and note the website address. Directions and worksheets are provided in this section to help you learn how to keep track of the resources you use for getting information.

NOTE TAKING
Notetaking is an important step in keeping track of answers and can be useful in helping you make meaningful connections. The worksheets in this section will give you some practice and tools to use in developing this skill.

CONNECTION MAKING
Making connections is taking information you learned, thinking about it deeply and connecting it to a purpose. The worksheets in this section guide this process.

EXPLORE ANSWERS & CONNECTIONS

COLLECT RESOURCES

One of the most important aspects of this step is keeping track of your resources in case you want to go back for more information and to give credit to the original resource. Any piece of information you learn from another source belongs to someone else and they should get the credit for the idea when you share your learning to an audience.

RESOURCE GUIDELINES
Begin the step of exploring answers and connections by learning how to record your resources. There are many different styles you can follow for citing your resources. The information collected about a resource is called a citation. When you share this information it is called citing a resource. This guide shows you a basic, simple style called MLA.

RESOURCES
This worksheet can be used to keep track of the resources you use to learn about your topic. Write down information about each of your resources using the guidelines provided or another citation style. Number these resources by putting a number in the box by each citation. Whenever you collect information from that resource, record the number in your notes or on a notecard so that you can remember where you found the information and give credit to that source.

EXPLORE ANSWERS & CONNECTIONS

RESOURCES GUIDELINES

Keep track of where you find information. Write down the resources using these guidelines. Number your resources and put the same number on any notes you take from that resource. That way you can be sure to cite where you found the information.

- BOOKS: Author (last name first) <u>Title (underlined)</u>. City where the book is published: Publisher, copyright date.

- MAGAZINES: Author (last name first). "Title of the article" (in quotation marks) <u>Title of the magazine (underlined)</u>. Date (day, month, year: Page numbers of the article.

- FILMS OR VIDEOS: <u>Title (underlined)</u>. Medium (ex. film, video). Production company, date. Time length. Web site if applicable.

- INTERVIEWS: Author (last name first). Type of interview. Date (day, month, year).

- WEB SITES: Author (last name first). Name of website. Web site address. Retrieved on: (day, month, year).

EXPLORE ANSWERS & CONNECTIONS

RESOURCES

EXPLORE ANSWERS & CONNECTIONS

NOTE-TAKING

Once you have collected some resources for learning about your topic, the next step is to begin learning and collecting information you can use for your own goals to solve a problem or to share with others. This section includes worksheets to help you learn a notetaking skill called nutshelling. It also includes worksheets for a collection grid and notecards.

NUTSHELLING

As you read or interview experts you will learn a lot of information. Rather than copying down every detail, you will want to summarize key information. Use the nutshelling worksheet to learn and practice this skill.

COLLECTION GRID

A collection grid can be a useful way to collect and record information you learn about your topic. Start by writing your questions in the first column. As you find answers, write them in the appropriate box in the answer column. Be sure to also record the number of the resource. You should have this recorded on the resource page on page 20, using the guidelines on page 19.

NOTECARDS

Remember I said this part of the process could be messy. Sometimes what you are learning is not as simple as asking questions and finding answers. Many times as you begin learning about a topic you find lots of interesting information but it doesn't really answer a particular question or there are lots of answers to consider. When this happens, notecards are often a better tool for collecting information. Use this worksheet and guidelines to give you some direction. Sticky notes can also be used and may be helpful if you plan to write a report. Then you can use the Stick It Research tools starting on page 44.

EXPLORE ANSWERS & CONNECTIONS

Note taking is an important skill in exploring answers. You can use the nutshelling strategy. All you need to do is read a paragraph and then try to summarize it in one sentence. Try it with these fun facts!

Gardening is a hobby many people do to grow food. Some people garden with large plots of land. Others garden with raised garden beds. Others garden with small pots. Gardens are grown by planting seeds and then taking care of the plants as they grow. Many people garden because they enjoy the process and eating the harvest.

Raising backyard chickens is a way to enjoy chickens as pets and enjoy fresh eggs. Chickens need a clean and safe area called a coop. They need fresh water to drink and grain to eat. One way to start a flock of chickens is by purchasing chicks. Young chicks need daily care to keep them warm, safe and fed. They grow very quickly and most breeds start laying eggs in about 5 months. You can usually expect about an egg a day from young, healthy chickens. In the winter months and as they age, chickens lay less eggs.

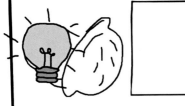

EXPLORE ANSWERS & CONNECTIONS

COLLECTION GRID

A collection grid is another way to keep track of answers to your questions and the source of the answer. In the first column, write your questions. When you find an answer, write it down in the answer column. Use the source column to write down the number of the resources from your resource page..

Question	Answer	Source

21

EXPLORE ANSWERS & CONNECTIONS

NOTECARDS

Your resources are recorded on your resource page. Use this box to write the number of the resource you are using for information on your notecard.

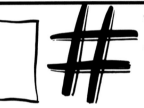

What's one or two words that sums up what this card is about? That's your hashtag!

Add key ideas you want to remember here. Put it in your own words if possible. Write down page numbers if it's from a printed source.

EXPLORE ANSWERS & CONNECTIONS

MAKE CONNECTIONS

When museum curators create an exhibit, they don't share every possible artifact. They select pieces to tell a story or to engage a particular audience. Think about what you have learned and a possible audience. You will explore audience more in the next step but for now it's helpful to have an idea of someone who might be interested in what you learned. If you used a collection grid you might just mark or highlight key information you want to share. If you collected notes using notecards or sticky notes you might want to have a little bit of fun getting messy. Take your notecards and try to organize them into piles based on the facts or information you collected. Give the pile a title. For example, if you were researching chickens and you wrote several notecards about what they eat, you could call this pile what chickens eat. You might try grouping your notes and creating titles in different ways until you find a connection you like. Once you have it organized how you want it, it is a good idea to hook your pile together with the title on top using a staple or paper clip. These piles are useful if you plan to share your learning in an essay, speech or poster.

Another way to make connections is to create a bubble brainstorm. To start, write your topic in the center of your paper. Now think about something you know about the topic and write it down in as few words possible and circle it. Think about something that gives more information about this idea and write it down in as few words as possible. Use lines and arrows to connect your different ideas. This is a map of everything you know about the topic. You can use it to share what you have learned or to identify areas where you might want to collect more information. Use the following pages to help you with your bubble brainstorm.

EXPLORE ANSWERS & CONNECTIONS

Use this worksheet to start your bubble brainstorm. Add your own bubbles and connectors to fit your information.

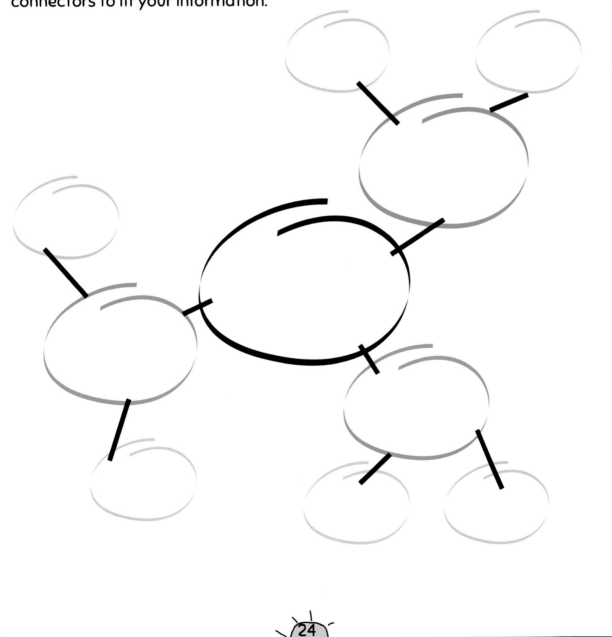

IDEAS
ANNOUNCE TO AN AUDIENCE

GETTING STARTED

One of the most exciting things about learning something is being able to share it with others or to use it to try to make the world better. The people you share what you learned with is your audience. This part of the process includes 3 steps: an audience brainstorm, creating a sharing plan and soliciting feedback.

AUDIENCE BRAINSTORM
Use this worksheet to identify possible audiences for your learning, ways to share what you have learned and how these audiences might benefit from what you share. This is a good time to think creatively. There are many and varied possible audiences and sharing options.

SHARING PLAN
Once you select an audience and a way to share your learning with that audience you want to create a plan for how to do it.

SOLICIT FEEDBACK
An audience can be a useful source for getting feedback about your project. You can use this information to improve your project or improve your skills for future projects. Use the worksheet to identify who to ask for feedback. There is also a template you can give to others for their feedback.

25

IDEAS

ANNOUNCE TO AN AUDIENCE

AUDIENCE BRAINSTORM

What did you learn? Who could benefit from that knowledge? Brainstorm possible audiences with whom you might want to share what you learned. Then brainstorm possible ways you can share your learning with them. Finally, think about how each audience might benefit from the information and project you share.

Audience	Ways to share information with the audience	How might the audience benefit from what you share?

 **IDEAS** # ANNOUNCE TO AN AUDIENCE

PRODUCT POSSIBILITIES

There are so many ways to share your project. Use this guide to help you brainstorm possibilities.

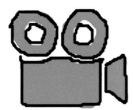 Multimedia

- Video
- Film/Movie
- Podcast
- Documentary
- Power Point

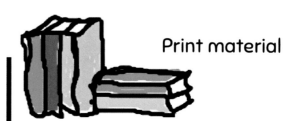 Print material

- Book
- Magazine or news article
- Blog
- Report
- Poem

 Visual arts

- Poster
- Board Game
- Collage
- Brochure
- Map
- Timeline
- Picture Book

 Presentation

- Dance
- Experiment
- TED talk
- Demonstration
- Speech

IDEAS ANNOUNCE TO AN AUDIENCE

SHARING PLAN

Select an audience and a way to share information from your brainstorm page. Use this sheet to plan how to announce your learning to an audience.

I think _____ need(s) to know about _____

audience   topic

I can share what I learned with _____

medium

Example: I think <u>gardeners</u> need to know about <u>collecting seeds</u>. I can share what I learned <u>with a</u> blog.

Here is a picture or description of my plan to announce to an audience.

ANNOUNCE TO AN AUDIENCE

SOLICIT FEEDBACK

Sharing your learning benefits others. They can learn from your experience and your ideas. Sharing to an audience also provides you with feedback to help you think more deeply about what you are learning, how you presented your material or to improve your learning process. The following questions can help you identify audiences who can provide you with feedback to help you improve.

List people you trust who can give you feedback about your project:

_____   _____

_____   _____

List people who might be experts or know more than you about your topic and can give you feedback about the information you shared and how you shared it:

_____   _____

_____   _____

List peers who can give you feedback about what you learned and your project:

_____   _____

_____   _____

When you ask for feedback it can be helpful to give people a way to share their responses. Solicit feedback by asking 2-3 people from your lists above to share feedback with you. You can invite them to use the form on the following page. Be sure to thank them for doing this for you. Use the feedback to make improvements in your project or to improve your learning process in the future.

IDEAS ANNOUNCE TO AN AUDIENCE

FEEDBACK FORM

Dear _____

Thank you for sharing your IDEAS with me. The part I liked best was

_____

_____

One habit or skill I noticed that you used is

_____

_____

I wonder

_____

_____

I enjoyed this project. One thing that might make it even better is

_____

_____

Thank you,

_____

SELF-REFLECT AND EVALUATE

GETTING STARTED

Learning doesn't just happen when you are doing something. Most learning happens when you think about what you have learned. This is called reflection. When you use criteria to evaluate the quality of something, that is called evaluation. Self-reflect and evaluate has 3 parts: evaluate using criteria, self-reflect and learning from mistakes.

EVALUATE USING CRITERIA
In school, projects and learning are often evaluated and given a grade. Grades are often based on some requirements or criteria. They are used to show how well you meet the criteria. While you don't need to grade your project, when you self-evaluate it can be helpful to identify some criteria you might use to determine the quality of your work. Remember how we used criteria in the beginning to help identify a topic. Evaluating using criteria is similar.

SELF-REFLECT
There are many different ways you can reflect. Here are a few suggestions:
- You can just sit and think.
- You can talk to someone about your project.
- You can draw pictures about what you learned.
- You can write about what you learned.
Use the self-reflect worksheet to guide you in reflecting about your IDEAS project, the process and what you learned about you.

LEARNING FROM MISTAKES
My mom always said, "he who makes no mistakes does nothing." I think she heard it somewhere but I'm not sure where. It's a good thing to remember when learning. We sometimes learn a lot from our mistakes. Use the Epic Fails worksheet to reflect on some of the mistakes you made in doing your IDEAS project.

IDEAS

SELF-REFLECT AND EVALUATE

EVALUATE USING CRITERIA

What are some of the many and varied criteria you can use to evaluate your project? For example, you may evaluate it based on neatness, on the quality of the information, or on how you displayed the information. Brainstorm some of the possibilities here:

Use your criteria to construct a rubric. Then use this rubric to evaluate your project.

Criteria	Ranking	Comments

IDEAS SELF-REFLECT AND EVALUATE

SELF-REFLECT

One of the key parts of learning is reflecting on what you have learned. It is important to think about the project but also about yourself and the process. Ask yourself – What did you learn about the topic? What did you learn about how you learn? What would you do differently next time? How will you improve the next time you learn? What did you enjoy learning or doing? Use this space to self-reflect. This is what I learned about:

- my IDEAS...

_____

_____

_____

- myself...

_____

_____

_____

- the process...

_____

_____

_____

IDEAS

Anyone who has never made a mistake has never tried anything new. –Albert Einstein

MY EPIC FAILS

SCAFFOLDS

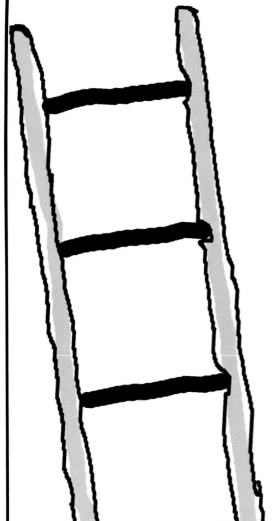

Sometimes you need a few extra tools to help you. Just like a ladder helps you reach higher places, scaffolds help you do more things. Check out these scaffolds and use the ones you need to help you do more with your IDEAS project.

Change the lightbulb – Use this scaffold if you think you need to change your IDEAS topic.

Playlist – As you are having fun with your IDEAS project, you can use the playlist to keep track of the steps.

Work Tracker – Use this sheet to keep track of your work, reflect and keep lists of things to do.

DASH – This is a quick version of IDEAS. This is good for getting a sense of what an IDEAS project is all about.

Stick It Research – If you use sticky notes or note cards to collect information you can use them with these sheets to build a rough draft of a research paper. Just stick them where they go and move them around until you have an order you like. This collection of tools will help you turn your IDEAS project into a written paper.

SCAFFOLDS

CHANGE THE LIGHTBULB

Sometimes IDEAS burn out, just like the lightbulbs in your house. Thomas Edison, the inventor of the lightbulb, tried over 100 things before he found the right way to make a lightbulb.

If your IDEAS project just doesn't seem to be working, it may be time to try a new one. Sometimes IDEAS are too big and you need to start small and take the next step. It may take you a few tries to get your IDEAS just right. Use this sheet to reflect on what is not working and what you can do to change it.

My IDEAS are not working because...

My next step is...

SCAFFOLDS

- [ ] IMAGINE POSSIBILITIES & IDENTIFY A TOPIC

- [ ] DEVELOP A LEARNING PLAN & QUESTIONS

- [ ] EXPLORE ANSWERS & CONNECTIONS

- [ ] ANNOUNCE TO AN AUDIENCE

- [ ] SELF-REFLECT & EVALUATE

SCAFFOLDS

Work Tracker

Date	Reflection	Tasks to Do
		• • • •
		• • • •
		• • • •
		• • • •
		• • • •

38

IDEAS - - - - DASH - - - - -

GETTING STARTED

After doing an IDEAS project, most students tell me they wish they had a better idea of the whole process before they started. I think part of the fun of doing an IDEAS project is the learning that happens along the way. There might be things you would have done differently, but that is part of the learning process. But, if you really want a quick way to get a sense of what an IDEAS project is like, you can do a DASH. A DASH is meant to be done quickly, usually in a class period or an hour or less. It can be done with any topic and it's great for teachers to use with something they want you to learn about anyway. The worksheets will guide you through each step of DASH. Here is a quick description of each step:

- Develop a learning plan and questions – Find some information about your topic. Think about what your class or other audience needs to know about the topic. Gather as much information as you can in about 15–20 minutes. Use the worksheet to record things you learn.

- Announce to an audience – Prepare an infographic or public service announcement to share the key things you learned with your class or other audience. This is a quick project and more of a sloppy copy than perfected work. Just focus on getting the key ideas communicated in a creative way.

- Self-reflect – Think about what you learned from this process. What was challenging? What was exciting? What did you learn about yourself as a learner? What did you learn about the topic?

- Highlight – Think about the process and key ideas that might help you when you do a full IDEAS project. Highlight things you want to remember to do or think about.

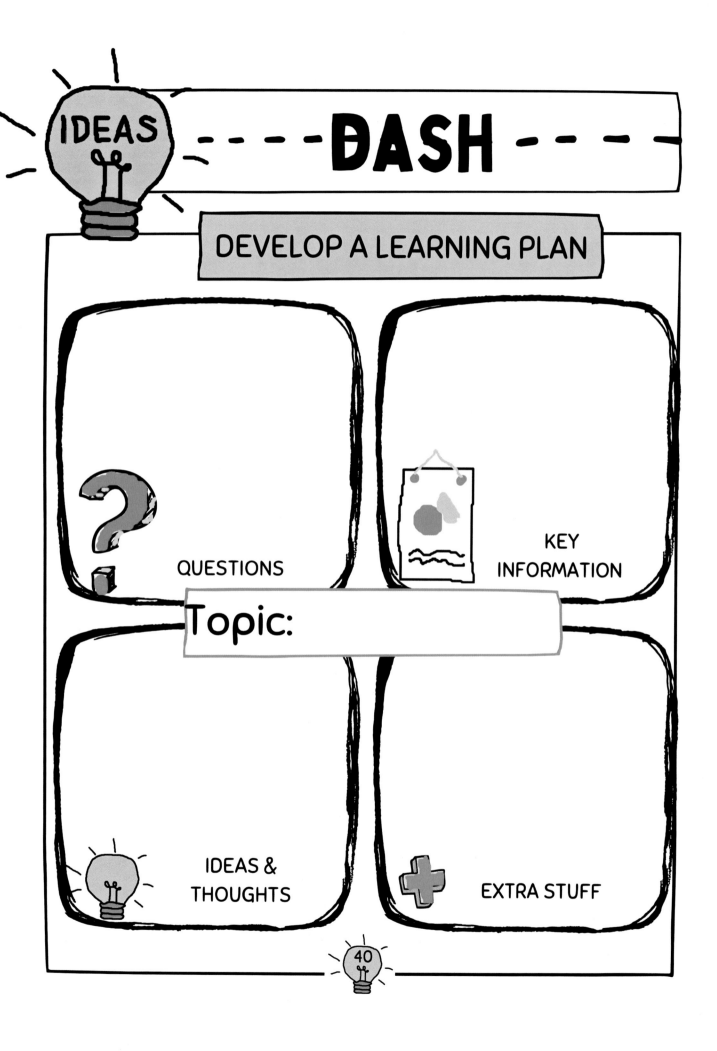

IDEAS DASH

DEVELOP A LEARNING PLAN

QUESTIONS

KEY INFORMATION

Topic:

IDEAS & THOUGHTS

EXTRA STUFF

40

IDEAS - - - - DASH - - - - -

ANNOUNCE TO AN AUDIENCE

Think about what you just learned about your topic. What does your class or maybe even the world, need to know about it. Use this space to create an infographic or write a public announcement to share the key things you learned. Have fun with it and make it creative.

IDEAS ----- DASH ----

SELF-REFLECT

One of the key parts of learning is reflecting on what you have learned. It is important to think about the project but also about yourself and the process. Ask yourself – What did you learn about the topic? What did you learn about how you learn? What would you do differently next time? How will you improve the next time you learn? What did you enjoy learning or doing? Use this space to self-reflect. This is what I learned about:

- my IDEAS...

- myself...

- the process...

IDEAS

DASH

HIGHLIGHT

List key things you learned from doing a DASH that might help you do an IDEAS project.

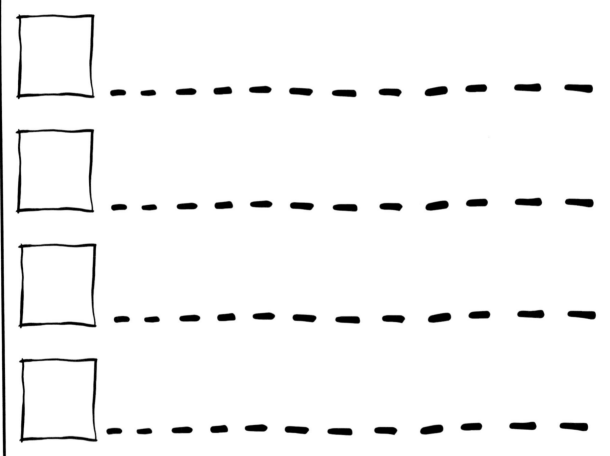

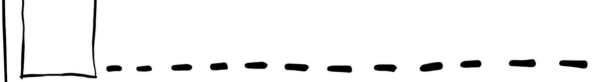

IDEAS

Stick It Research

GETTING STARTED

While there are many different ways to share what you have learned, one of the basic ways students are asked to share information they have learned is with a research paper. It is a written piece of work which usually includes an introduction, body and conclusion. Depending on the instructor, there may be different styles and requirements for a research paper. The following pages will provide you with supports to help you write your own research paper. You can use this checklist to keep track of the parts you have completed.

☐ Hook your readers: A good paper and a good paragraph starts with a hook, something that catches your readers attention and gets them interested in reading your paper. Use this worksheet to get some practice with hooks and write your own.

☐ Write a thesis. A thesis is a statement that tells your audience what your paper is about. It is also used to provide the main idea of a paragraph. Use this worksheet to learn about writing a thesis statment and then write your own.

☐ Create clever conclusions. Paragraphs and papers need an ending. Learn some different ways to conclude your paper and write your own conclusion.

☐ Use sticky notes or note cards you collected to build your paper. This is a great way to start because you can easily move things around and change it without having to rewrite things. Use the worksheets as a guide.

☐ Add transitions. As you write your paper, just follow your sticky notes. Use the transition worksheet to add interesting transition words.

☐ Put it all together. Check out this example of how all the sticky note facts were pulled together into a paper. Now you try.

Stick It Research

HOOK YOUR READERS

Good writers have interesting introductions as their very first sentence! Catch your reader's attention by writing a hook!

TYPES OF HOOKS

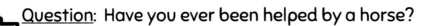

Question: Have you ever been helped by a horse?

Onomatopeia: Giddy up! I rode off down the trail.

Dialogue: "I want to ride a horse!" he yelled.

Setting: The dark, green grasses swayed along the trail.

Fact: Children need practice to learn how to ride a horse.

Funny: Have you ever seen a horsefly?

WRITE YOUR OWN HOOK

IDEAS

Stick It Research

THESIS STATEMENT RULES

- Provides readers with the main claim of your paper. It tells the readers what your paper is about.
- Makes a claim that others may either agree or disagree with.
- Is a statement, rather than a question.
- Is written in your own words. It is not a quote from a source.

THESIS CRITIQUE

Read the following thesis examples. Cross out the ones that do not fit the rules. What makes a good thesis statement?
- Horseback riding is a great way to improve physical and mental health.
- Kids ride on horse trails or in arenas.
- Horseback riding is fun.
- Students should wear cowboy boots to school.
- Cowboy hats are ugly.
- Video games may be linked to an increase in violence.
- Video games are awesome.
- Spiderman is my favorite character.
- I love to ride horses.
- Do you ride horses?

WRITE YOUR OWN THESIS

IDEAS

Stick It Research

CLEVER CONCLUSIONS

Good writers have clever conclusions at the end of their writing.

TYPES OF CONCLUSIONS

Feeling: Horseback riders are the happiest athletes on earth.

Question: Do you think you will ever go horseback riding?

Lesson: It is always a good idea to bring a helmet when riding.

Advice: You should consider going horseback riding more often.

Fact: Children need practice to learn how to ride a horse..

WRITE YOUR OWN CONCUSION

Stick It Research

1–Grabbing Sentence

Catch the attention of your audience with a fun fact, a question or an interesting statement.

Example:
Did you know horses can help humans heal?

2 – Thesis statement

Tell what you are writing about in a clear sentence.

Example:
Equine therapy is used to help people overcome fears or difficult emotions.

3 – Framing Sentence

Let your reader know what you will be telling them about This will be the body of the paper.

Example:
The special relationship people have with horses and the activities they do with them is what makes this therapy work.

4 – Optional closing

Add a sentence to end your introductory paragraph.

Example:
When people work with their therapist and a horse, they can often work through what is bothering them.

48

IDEAS

Stick It Research

1–Thesis Sentence

Tell the audience what the paragraph will be about.

Example:
Horses and humans have a special relationship.

2 – Supporting Facts

Share facts or details that support your thesis.

Example:
When horses trust somone they are loyal and affectionate (2).

3 – Supporting Facts

Share facts or detalis that support your thesis.

Example:
They can read human emotions and detect fear (1).

4 –Facts or closing

Add additional details or close your paragraph.

Example:
These characteristics of horses are helpful to clients in therapy.

Stick It Research

BODY PLANNING PAGE – 2

1–Thesis Sentence

Tell the audience what the paragraph will be about.

Example:
Building a trusting relationship with a horse comes from groundwork.

2 – Supporting Facts

Share facts or details that support your thesis.

Example:
In equine therapy, the client does not ride, groom or feed the horses (2)

3 – Supporting Facts

Share facts or detalis that support your thesis.

Example:
Instead, the client interacts with the horse in a natural setting with the guidance of a therapist.

4 –Facts or closing

Add additional details or close your paragraph.

Example:
These groundwork activities help the clients work through their fears or emotions with the horses help,.

Stick It Research

CONCLUSION PLANNING PAGE

1–Reminding Sentence

Restate your initial grabbing sentence.

Example:
Horses have a unique ability to help humans process feelings and heal.

2 – Thesis statement

Remind your audience what the essay was about in a clear sentence.

Example:
They are used in equine therapy to help people who are sad or hurt.

3 – Framing Sentence

Remind your reader what you shared in the body of the essay.

Example:
The characteristics of horses and the activies used are important parts of equine therapy.

4 – Optional closing

Add a concluding statement or question.

Example:
Horses are amazing animals and now we know that with equine therapy, they can even help people heal.

IDEAS

Stick It Research

TRANSITIONS

Good writer use transition words to signal changes between ideas, to show location, to show time, to indicate more information, or to conclude a piece of writing.

SEQUENCE OR TRANSITION

- first...second...third
- in the first place...also...lastly
- after
- afterward
- as soon as
- at first
- at last
- before
- before long
- finally
- in the meantime
- later
- meanwhile
- next
- soon
- then

TIME

- while
- meanwhile
- soon
- then
- after
- second
- today
- later
- next
- afterward
- as soon as
- before
- when suddenly
- during
- until
- finally

LOCATION

- above
- across
- around
- behind
- beside
- between
- in back of
- in front of
- inside
- near
- outsie
- over
- under

MORE INFORMATION

- besides
- furthermore
- in addition
- in fact

CONCLUSION

- in conclusion
- finally
- lastly
- to sum up

52

IDEAS

Stick It Research

Horses Heal with Equine Therapy

Introduction

Did you know horses can help humans heal? Equine therapy is used to help people overcome fears or difficult emotions.The special relationship people have with horses and the activities they do with them is what makes this therapy work. When people work with their therapist and a horse, they can often work through what is bother them.

Body

Horses and humans have a special relationship. When horses trust someone they are loyal and affectionate (1). They can read human emotions and detect fear (2). These characteristics of horses are helpful to clients in therapy.

Building a trusting relationship with a horse comes from groundwork. In equine therapy, the client does not ride, groom or feed the horses (1). Instead, the client interacts with the horse in a natural setting with the guidance of a therapist. These groundwork activities help the clients work through their fears or emotions with the horses help (1).

Conclusion

Horses have a unique ability to help humans process feelings and heal. They are used in equine therapy to help people who are sad or hurt. The characteristics of horses and the activities used are important parts of equine therapy. Horses are amazing animals and now we know that with equine therapy, they can even help people heal.

Resources

Works Cited:
1. Clark, Jodi. (2021). Using Equine Therapy as Mental Health Treatment. https://www.verywellmind.com/equine-therapy-mental-health-treatment-4177932 Retrieved on March 22, 2022.
2. Idaho Youth Ranch. (2022). Understanding Equine Therapy. https://www.youthranch.org/understanding-equine-therapy. Retrieved on March 22, 2022.

RESOURCES

BOOKS TO INSPIRE YOU

Yamada, Kobi. What Do You Do with an Idea? Library Ideas, LLC, 2021.

Yamada, Kobi. What Do You Do with a Problem? Library Ideas, LLC, 2021.

RESOURCES THAT INSPIRED ME

Johnson, Nancy L. The Quick Question Workbook. Pieces of Learning, 1999.

Kemper, Dave, and Chris Krenzke. Writers Express: A Handbook for Young Writers, Thinkers, and Learners. Write Source, 2000.

Spencer, John. "What Is Inquiry-Based Learning?" YouTube, 5 Dec. 2017, https://youtu.be/QlwkerwaV2E.

ABOUT THE AUTHOR

Cheryl Peterson, Ph.D. created IDEAS in 1992 and has been continuously improving it ever since. Countless students and teachers have had amazing learning experiences with IDEAS! She loves to engage students in learning with play, practice and purpose. Cheryl has taught at multiple grade levels and settings including public schools, homeschool co-ops and college. She started her career in teaching with a BA Degree in Elementary Education. Wanting to learn more she continued her education and received a MA in Educational Psychology from the University of Iowa. She lived the inquiry process working on her doctorate degree in Curriculum and Instruction at the University of Minnesota. She has spent much of her career as a gifted specialist and has taught for 6 years in the Gifted Certificate Program at Hamline University. Cheryl lives with her husband, Darrin, and kids, Elena and Ben, in Illinois where she also takes care of a garden, chickens, horses, cats and a dog. She is constantly inspired by her farm and family to ask questions, learn more and try new things.

Connect with Cheryl Peterson at drcherylpeterson.com

Teachers can join her IDEAS group and share strategies and insights at

Made in the USA
Columbia, SC
29 October 2022

69849093R00035